The Woman Who Thought She Had It All

GETTING MONEY

by

Patricia Bailey

Gotham Books

30 N Gould St.
Ste. 20820, Sheridan, WY 82801
https://gothambooksinc.com/

Phone: 1 (307) 464-7800

© 2024 *Patricia Bailey*. All rights reserved.

No part of this book may be reproduced, stored in a retrieval system, or transmitted by any means without the written permission of the author.

Published by Gotham Books (March 6, 2024)

ISBN: 979-8-88775-505-2 (P)
ISBN: 979-8-88775-506-9 (E)

Because of the dynamic nature of the Internet, any web addresses or links contained in this book may have changed since publication and may no longer be valid.

The views expressed in this work are solely those of the author and do not necessarily reflect the views of the publisher, and the publisher hereby disclaims any responsibility for them.

Harmony, a woman hailing from the aristocratic district, was born and raised there with her three children. Despite being surrounded by four sisters and three brothers, she struggled to grasp the essential values of life, leading her to adopt a relentless and fast-paced approach to everything she did. Known throughout town for her involvement in activities such as gambling, managing two businesses, networking, and advertising, Harmony drove a luxurious 2024 BMW convertible, earning her the nickname "money getting red."

Charging a hefty fee of $500 for a massage, Harmony's friend questioned the rationale behind such a steep price. Perhaps there was more to it than just monetary gain. It appeared that Harmony was grappling with a lack of morals and self-respect, possibly due to her failure to recognize her true worth as a phenomenal woman. It became evident that Harmony was in dire need of inner strength and support to navigate through life's challenges and rediscover her values.

Harmony is a mother of three striving to achieve a better life for herself. She believed that hustling was the only way to elevate herself, unaware of any other path to success. Feeling overwhelmed, Harmony sought solace in her friend Mahogany, the only person she felt comfortable confiding in besides God. With tears in her eyes, Harmony expressed her exhaustion with her current lifestyle, characterized by being taken advantage of by various individuals.

Despite Mahogany's loyal friendship, Harmony failed to grasp the true essence of companionship. In her efforts to impart wisdom on the values of life and friendship to Mahogany, Harmony overlooked the reciprocal nature of their relationship. When questioned by Mahogany about her understanding of friendship, Harmony admitted her ignorance on the matter. It became evident that Harmony had much to learn about the true meaning of friendship from her steadfast companion Mahogany.

I would like to address the issue at hand as I feel there has been a lack of honesty in our friendship. Mahogany retrieved a dictionary from her pocketbook and looked up the definition of true friendship.

The definition of a true friend is an individual who consistently supports you, looks out for your well-being, and ensures you are not in harm's way. They never intentionally guide you towards decisions that are detrimental to your best interests. A true friend always prioritizes your welfare. Lately, I have noticed a lack of this level of support from you, and if you are unable to uphold the true essence of friendship as I have described, I would prefer not to associate with someone exhibiting such characteristics.

In response, Harmony stated that her primary focus is on financial gain and that I am hindering her progress. Therefore, as of today, our friendship is terminated. Mahogany was disheartened by the turn of events. Mahogany was more deeply pained than words can express as she walked away, tears streaming down her cheeks. However, she found herself compelled to demonstrate tough love in the face of the situation. Their friendship had roots dating back to their kindergarten days; in fact, she was Mahogany's sole confidante. As she parted ways, she uttered the words, "I must recognize my own value. One cannot transform a promiscuous individual into a committed partner; she will always remain true to her nature. Therefore, you may continue down your current path." With a heavy heart, Mahogany departed, reflecting, "I must exercise discretion in selecting my companions. Understanding one's self-worth is paramount. Self-preservation and a true sense of identity are critical, and I sincerely hope for her well-being." Each passing day found Mahogany contemplating Harmony with great frequency. She understood that the trajectory Harmony was on could lead to incarceration, injury, or worse. While Mahogany desires the best for her friend, the reality of the situation remains unchanged. . As Harmony asserts, she endeavors to live life to its fullest and achieve all that is within her capacity, until one fateful day when she becomes embroiled in a serious dispute with a former female associate. Referred to as Big Sarge, this individual harbored deep feelings for Harmony, who, in turn, desired to distance herself from her prior lifestyle. Coming to terms with her bisexuality, Harmony ultimately uncovered her true identity. Her heart longed to be united with Musa in matrimony. Despite being habitually inebriated and reliant on alcohol from dawn till dusk, Harmony frequented the streets in a state of intoxication. Deluded into believing she had attained the pinnacle of success and contentment, she soon realized that, upon shutting the doors behind her, she was left alone with her thoughts. Despite amassing wealth through illicit activities and providing massages, Harmony found herself devoid of genuine happiness. She became accustomed to seeking validation from others while battling to cultivate self-love, realizing that the material wealth she had amassed was fleeting. Thus, Harmony embarked on her journey towards self-discovery and fulfillment. Engaging in introspection on the transient nature of her possessions, Harmony contemplated her future with optimism. She acknowledged that despite holding a high school diploma, she had the opportunity to return to college and pursue a new path. Contemplating her options, she considered investing her resources wisely to attain success.

As an aspiring entrepreneur, Harmony envisioned the establishment of a physical therapy center where she could offer massages and therapy services. With aspirations of expanding her venture into a thriving business, she planned to obtain expertise in business management and accounting to complement her skills as a physical therapist.

Determined to achieve her goals, Harmony set out to explore potential locations for her future enterprise. Grateful for the educational foundation provided by her high school diploma, she began researching schools offering programs in massage therapy. With unwavering determination, Harmony embarked on her journey towards building her own massage and therapy center from scratch.

I have devised a plan and am now ready to pursue my career. I deeply regret my previous behavior, as it was fueled by frustration and uncertainty. Although we have never celebrated holidays or special occasions together, I am feeling exhausted. Despite our agreement to not develop romantic feelings, it is apparent that it is time for us to move forward and establish a relationship.

As we strive towards our individual goals, I realize that you have always been a part of my plans. I regret not taking action sooner and should have acted upon your sister's advice. Harmony, having completed her appointment at the health department, seemed prepared for a new chapter with her soon-to-be partner.

Musa greeted her with a smile and declared, "You are my future wife." Although hesitant at first, Harmony felt a sense of anticipation and excitement for the journey ahead. I no longer need to contemplate the matter. As Harmony responded, I am prepared to progress. It is time for me to settle down. I have always desired a large family and a beautiful home. We currently have three children, unless you desire to have three more. Harmony remarked that three plus three has always equated to six, and adding three more would result in a considerable number of mouths to feed. I am still youthful. Harmony suggested perhaps in five years, when I am thirty years old.

Harmony responded, "Let us proceed cautiously. You are moving too swiftly. Allow me to complete my education first. I am determined to adhere to my long- and short-term objectives; it is imperative." Musa assured Harmony, "You are not alone in this endeavor; we will face it together as a united front." Harmony, we shall commence the search for a new residence next week. Do you have any specific preferences in mind? What size of home are you considering?" Are you interested in acquiring the house? Would you prefer a single-level residence or a two-story home? Please provide a detailed description of your preferences. I personally favor a rural setting as it would allow us to use four-wheelers, which the boys would greatly enjoy. By purchasing 100 acres of land, we could construct multiple dwellings and even establish an RV park, thus creating generational wealth. As the children grow older, we could also incorporate tiny homes into the property. It is my vision to establish a family-run business, with you and the children managing the RV park. This venture will require initial investment, but I am confident in its potential for success. This endeavor will not only bring financial prosperity, but also valuable life skills to the children. I envision Mickey overseeing the front desk, while Al and Tony assist you with various tasks on the premises. We may need to hire additional staff to support this operation, considering the scale of our plans.

On a vast expanse of land containing numerous small homes, it will be necessary for someone to oversee the maintenance of the campgrounds. This includes the upkeep of the septic tank, management of the office, handling deliveries, and keeping track of inventory. Running a business of this nature requires significant effort, and we will be conducting thorough screenings of all individuals who visit the premises.

This precaution is important to me, as we have our children on site and a multitude of unfamiliar guests arriving to camp. It is imperative that we have some knowledge of those who come through our doors, as you rightly pointed out, Musa. Tomorrow, we will officially acquire these 100 acres of land. After much searching, a young man has agreed to assist me in cleaning the grounds and laying the groundwork for the small homes.

Our primary residence will be a 4900 square-foot home, serving as the main building on the property. The front office will be located at the forefront, while our living quarters will be situated at the rear. The residence is secluded, off the grid, and will be meticulously designed with your unique taste in decor. It is evident that you possess a discerning eye for aesthetics. I believe this project is a well-thought-out strategy. Our children are now of working age, and considering Micky's 19 years of age, her exceptional skills make her a suitable candidate to manage the front office efficiently. Her height ensures that no detail will escape her notice. Additionally, with Al aged 18 and Tony aged 20, they could pursue further education in accounting. Tony's passion for mathematics makes him a perfect fit for this field. His ambition to construct and build the universe aligns well with professions such as construction, building maintenance electricians, and other related areas. Obtaining my black seal certification is crucial for ensuring comprehensive coverage in all aspects. Musa, as a retired veteran, you play a vital role in my long-established plan, meticulously crafted in my thoughts over time. I have served in the military. What I require is a supportive woman by my side, who will stand strong. Therefore, I kindly ask you to reduce the amount of alcohol consumption. I am not insisting on complete abstinence.

As everyone deserves to revel in life's pleasures, I suggest we limit our celebrations to weekends. Do you concur with this proposal, my dear? As I will be fully occupied with my studies and various responsibilities, I appreciate your understanding at this time. While we may not always see eye to eye, I am confident that we can find common ground and resolve any differences.

I am grateful to have you by my side. I am no longer concerned about other women, as you are my queen, my pride, my joy, and my everything. Musa confided in Harmony, expressing his joy in finding the woman of his dreams, and his commitment to loving her wholeheartedly. Shall we set a date for our engagement party? This event promises to be of great interest and significance to us all. I have never before shared such intimate thoughts and feelings with anyone, but I feel compelled to do so now with Harmony. vow to love you unconditionally and give you my unwavering support always. Nothing and no one will ever come between us. As we prepare to exchange our vows and establish open lines of communication, Musa suggests that we schedule regular discussions every Friday to share our thoughts, concerns, preferences, and dislikes.

We will approach these conversations with our best efforts and draw upon our knowledge and experience. Harmony, I observed that you did not disclose the details of your doctor's visit. Is there something you need to tell me? I urge you to be transparent about any issues that arose during your appointment.

Furthermore, I must inform you that I am pregnant. Despite this development, I am determined to persevere as a strong, independent woman. I am committed to completing my education, launching new business ventures, and supporting you in achieving your goals. going to love you unconditionally.

Musa has graciously responded to Harmony's proposal for this day, and together we are planning the most grand engagement party imaginable. A few of my esteemed military colleagues will be in attendance, adding to the festivity of the occasion. Additionally, I am excited to announce that I will be hosting an extravagant bachelor party, ensuring that this celebration will be one to remember.

Furthermore, it has been decided that Harmony will arrange her bridal shower to coincide with this special day. Harmony, you have captured my heart since the moment I first saw you, and I am eager to lay bare my thoughts, emotions, and spirit to you. I vow to be completely open and honest with you, giving you all that I am.

In pledging myself completely to you, Harmony, I mean to convey that our love and commitment will remain steadfast and unwavering. Our union will be free from any external influences or distractions, as we come together every Friday to reflect on our journey together. Rest assured, my beloved, we are in perfect accord, and our love will only continue to grow stronger with each passing day. Harmony has begun to open up and express herself, and I am grateful for the opportunity to share this deep connection with her. As time progressed, Musa commenced the management of his business endeavors. However, he initiated his efforts at the campground. His intention is to develop accommodations for 40 tiny homes on the premises, which will cater to mothers and children. Additionally, he plans to inaugurate the RV park within a span of four months. There exists a considerable number of individuals worldwide who possess the capacity to aid the homeless population significantly.

We intend to offer meal programs for children as well as educational initiatives for parents who are facing challenges in obtaining a high school diploma and pursuing further education.

This initiative serves as an excellent starting point for mothers to rekindle their love for their children and establish a secure household. By the time they depart, they will have the means to live independently and achieve the majority of their short and long-term objectives. Ideally, upon leaving our facility, they will have progressed to such an extent that a return becomes unnecessary.

This initiative presents an exceptional opportunity for individuals to embark on a fresh start. After the lapse of four months, Musa successfully realized the establishment of the RV. The park appears quite picturesque with the 50 acres of land now fully occupied by small, quaint homes. Interviews for potential households will commence on Monday. We will initiate the process with the Department of Social Services (DSS) to facilitate the transfer of households and commence our record checks. Come Monday morning, Harmony and Musa will commence interviewing and conducting record checks. The first batch of ten individuals is scheduled to arrive on Monday morning. Among them, one woman is accompanied by two unaccounted-for children, which presents a potential complication due to her past record. Kim is diligently working towards resolving this issue.

The expungement process will be undertaken in due course. Harmony assists the young woman with two children in finding temporary accommodation until her situation stabilizes. I believe there may be vacancies at another shelter; allow me to verify this information. Your patience is appreciated as I strive to secure a suitable residence that accommodates a mother and her four children.

Kim, we have a spot reserved for you here. Currently, four of the tiny homes are occupied by mothers and children, which is a positive development. Moving forward, we can begin implementing various programs such as parenting, housing, vocational, childcare, and aftercare. It will be essential to conduct orientation sessions to assess the educational level of these women.

Our program will consist of three phases, with families gaining full access to the homes after completing phase 3. They will be required to establish a bank account with a minimum balance of $5,000. Upon completion of the program, families will have access to Section 8 housing and job opportunities.

This will provide a stable foundation for these families to rebuild their lives. Expungement has been approved, allowing you to move into the tiny homes with your children. After six months, Harmony will be able to provide additional support for you and your family. Your dedication to completing all three phases will set you on the path towards a brighter future. As we begin this journey together, I invite you to take a moment to reflect on who you are and what your children mean to you. This assignment is a chance for you to share your story, and it will be a part of your grade for phase 1. I know it may seem daunting, but I believe in each and every one of you.

Take your time with this task, and feel free to connect with your fellow classmates. Tomorrow is a new day, and we will take things one step at a time. The first day of orientation is complete, and I hope you all have a wonderful day. Remember, lunch is at 12 and dinner is at 6. Please take your paperwork with you and return it on Monday.

I want to wish you all a fantastic rest of the week. I am excited to see you all around campus and get to know each of you better. Remember, we are all in this together. Good morning everyone! Let's start our day with a prayer as soon as we wake up. Who here knows the serenity prayer? If you don't know it, don't worry, I'll make sure to provide a copy for you before we start our day. I encourage each of you to join me in repeating after me:

"God, grant me the serenity to accept the things I cannot change, the courage to change the things I can, and the wisdom to know the difference. Remember, there are things in life that we cannot control, but we can ask God for courage and understanding. Let's pray for strength to face these challenges. And remember, we also have the power to change the things we can. Let's strive to be the best version of ourselves in all that we do.

Believe in yourself, have the courage to face your challenges, and trust that God will guide and support you along the way. You have the strength and capability to achieve anything you set your mind to. Remember to have the wisdom to discern between what you can change and what you cannot. By understanding this distinction, you will be able to focus on improving what you can and accepting what you cannot change.

Pray for the courage to make necessary changes in your life, to fix what is not right. Trust that God will be there to support and guide you, especially during your most challenging moments.

Seek serenity in accepting the things that cannot be changed, and ask for insight to distinguish between the two.

As you work on accepting what cannot be changed, know that God will place it in your heart and provide you with the guidance you need. Listen for His voice and follow His lead. Let harmony flow through your family relationships, and close with a prayer for guidance and support as you lead them. Stretch your hands out to God, for He is your ultimate source of help. Trust in His guidance and blessings for yourself and your loved ones. Dear God, I humbly beseech you to assist me in leading these families to a higher understanding, revealing to them your divine presence. I trust that you will not burden them beyond their capabilities. Though they may currently lack comprehension, grant them the wisdom, knowledge, and insight necessary to navigate their circumstances. Aid me in facilitating the transition for these families to achieve independence in their own residences. Please help them maintain focus throughout the three phases of this transformative process. Additionally, as these women embark on the challenging path to success, I implore you to offer them guidance and support. Enable them to reconcile their roles as mothers and wives while pursuing their aspirations.

Provide guidance for their children, showing them the path to a fulfilling and righteous life. We seek your assistance in ensuring these children understand that their struggles are ending and that help is forthcoming. Lastly, grant me the clarity and direction needed to administer this program according to your will. We offer our gratitude and praise for your blessings. Amen. these things in your name, amen!!!!!! Amen Ladies, I want you to know we are all in this together. Anything you need to know, don't hesitate to ask Harmony, saying to herself. Help in these families will strengthen their minds. Each one teaches one in my mind the struggle I went through to get where I am now. I thank you for every blessing you stored, and dear God please help give these women's strength to elevate to the next level. Help these women to be successful, and Harmony is praying to herself. Knowing she has a process as well as going to school for massage therapy, cosmetology, business, and administration, we will be successful as she walked out the door with the families and smiled, saying God would not put anything on me. I can't bear. I believe, and I want you ladies to believe that I will see all of you ladies by 12 noon. Dear Ladies,

I humbly ask for your attention as we gather in prayer. Let us come together in unity, seeking strength and guidance in the name of the Lord. Harmony, with a heart full of compassion, encourages us to support one another and share our knowledge. It is through this support that we will empower our minds and uplift our spirits.

As we reflect on our own journeys and the challenges we have faced, let us be grateful for the blessings that have been bestowed upon us. Let us seek God's grace and mercy to help us overcome our struggles and reach new heights of success. Harmony, with her dedication to education and self-improvement, serves as an example of perseverance and determination.

As we depart to face the day ahead, let us carry with us the belief that God will not burden us with more than we can bear. Let us trust in His plan for us and have faith that He will guide us towards a brighter future. I urge you, my dear ladies, to join me in the main dorm at noon, where we will come together as a family and share a meal in unity.

With warm regards and prayers for our collective success, I am in need of the assistance of three women for a specific job assignment. Rhonda, Margo, and Rachelle, I request your presence. Your task will involve managing breakfast, lunch, and dinner arrangements. Additionally, I am seeking four more individuals to join me once additional residences are operational. I am looking for a team of housekeepers to fulfill this role. Your participation in this responsibility is based on the skills you have acquired and the certifications you have obtained. Please consider it as a professional trade, and you will be compensated accordingly. Collaboration is essential in this endeavor. It is important to note that while everyone is responsible for making their own beds, you ladies are tasked with collecting and disposing of all waste. Detailed schedules and locations will be provided for you. Brenda, Maia, Maria, and Kia, I am requesting your assistance. I would be happy to give you a tour around campus. It's important to know where the dumpster is located and where the cleaning supplies will be kept so that we can all work together to keep germs at bay. I will check everything at the end of the day to make sure it's all clean. I understand that it may not seem like much, but everyone will still have their privacy. Please don't feel discouraged - just set the trash by the door and the girls will take care of it. All windows will be open, and the central air will be on to keep each tiny home clean and free of debris. Make sure to keep things organized under the beds, hang coats on the coat rack, and line up shoes on the shoe rack.

After the third phase, you will be allowed to have weekend company in the guest house of the tiny homes on the east side of campus. Unfortunately, we do not allow family members on the west side of campus, but only households that reside here. As I show you around the campus, I receive a phone call from Mahogany.

Mahogany II hope this message finds you well. I wanted to take a moment to express how much I miss you and how grateful I am for your presence in my life. As we prepare for our upcoming trip to Jamaica, I am filled with emotions reflecting on our journey together. I believe it is crucial for us to set aside seven days next month too, share our thoughts and feelings, and strengthen our bond.

I want you to know that I value our relationship deeply, and I am committed to ensuring that nothing will ever come between us again. Your support and companionship mean everything to me, and I am truly grateful for your presence in my life.

On a personal note, I have some exciting news to share with you. I am currently five months pregnant with Musa's baby, and we have recently purchased an RV park and 100 acres of land where we have set up tiny homes. Additionally, I am in the process of planning to open a headquarters center on the property.

I am looking forward to sharing all of these developments with you and continuing to build our bond. Your friendship and guidance have been invaluable to me, and I am eager to hear your thoughts and opinions on these new ventures.

Thank you for always being there to listen and support me. I am excited for our upcoming trip to Jamaica and the opportunity to reconnect and strengthen our relationship. women who will resign from the RV park. These women will accomplish everything in three phases. If you would like, you can start working for me, and you can live in one of the tiny homes to be able to stack your money. I think that would be a great thing, as weeks and weeks go by and all the women are accomplishing everything they need to accomplish. Everyone is in phase 1, and on Mondays, a GED program will start. We will also have cooking classes for those who do not know how to cook. We will also have sewing classes, and everyone will get certificates for all the jobs that they do in detail. We will also have agriculture classes for those who would like to plant vegetables and make a garden. Having that self- preservation is the first thing—believing in yourself and knowing how to run your home. And providing for yourself with these skills, I'm providing for these ladies is for them to be able to live on their own. During a conversation, Mahogany inquired of Harmony the inspiration behind the establishment of the RV park. Harmony responded, stating that her personal journey and achievements had motivated her to create a space where women worldwide could come together to discover their self-worth. She emphasized the importance of self-love and self-preservation, highlighting that material possessions do not equate to inner fulfillment. Harmony expressed her desire to empower women by guiding them from the bottom to the top, setting goals, and fostering resilience. Building self-confidence and self-esteem in women held significant value for her, as she aimed to assist ten women at a time in achieving personal growth and success. Additionally, Harmony mentioned a game of "left-right center" at the RV park, which serves as a fun way to engage in a money-making activity. She advised using dice for the game, ensuring that each player had at least five ones to participate. Scared money? It's okay, we all have our worries. But remember, sometimes you have to take risks to see rewards. You know how I am; she says with a smile. Mahogany, would you like to try these new gummies? We've been friends since we were kids, so if I'm going to try them, it's only right I do it with you. How will they affect you? It's hard to say, we all react differently. Let's find out together. Musa is here to witness it all. Harmony, I'll go with the red one, you said the green one is the best. Tonight is couple's night and we'll be playing that game, let's hope we don't have any unexpected reactions. The guests are arriving, each couple bringing their own dirt bikes. I've never ridden one before, but tonight I'm going to give it a try. Mike and Shaheed have the coolest custom-made bikes in town. Brian and Tyson also have custom bikes, but not as impressive. Musa has never had ridden a dirt bike, but he sure is going to experience that shit today. Come on, guys, before the ladies come out. Well, I can show you how to ride and give you a lesson for about an hour. Everyone rides around the block on the dirt bikes, splashing mud and water everywhere. It's your turn, Musa may have been confident in his ability to ride a dirt bike, but today he was in for a challenging experience. With a sense of urgency, he urged his friends to hurry up before the women joined them. Offering to provide a one-hour lesson on riding, Musa led the group around the block on their dirt bikes, creating a trail of mud and water in their wake.

When it was Musa's turn to ride, he boasted about his experience with a 1200 motorcycle, claiming that riding a dirt bike would be a breeze for him. However, his overconfidence led to a comical mishap as he lost control of the bike, crashing and injuring himself in the process.

Harmony's reaction was one of disbelief and concern, questioning why Musa had attempted to ride without proper knowledge or skill. As Musa sat crying by the car, Harmony retreated to the porch to discuss the incident with Mahogany. No one understands Harmony; she knows that she is not going to ever eat another edible ever again. Harmony immediately called for emergency medical assistance, and the ambulances arrived promptly. Musa was unable to move his right side, causing Harmony great distress. As the situation unfolded, a sense of panic set in as the effects of the edible began to intensify for both of them. Harmony found herself overwhelmed, experiencing hallucinations and erratic behavior, but managed to regain composure before the ambulance arrived. In a moment of clarity, she expressed gratitude for their safety. Despite the chaotic events, Harmony made a vow to never consume edibles again. Finally, the ambulance arrived, and Musa's distress was evident as he expressed his inability to move his right side and the feeling that something was seriously wrong. The ambulance has arrived, with the medical team quickly pulling out the stretcher. Musa asked about the current president, stating that it is Tuesday and Biden is our president, as he was being placed on the stretcher by the ambulance crew. Without a neck brace, Musa was rushed to the trauma room for evaluation by the physicians who ordered X-rays. It was determined that Musa had broken two collarbones, three ribs, and had cracked both legs, causing disorientation. As we waited at the hospital, we prayed for Musa's recovery, trusting in the power of the Almighty. Harmony reassured Musa to believe and stay strong, promising to be there by his side as he was prepared for emergency surgery. As Musa drifted off under anesthesia, he reflected on his inner struggles of self-acceptance and identity. Juggling conflicting aspects of himself, he found it challenging to navigate through his thoughts. I hope that Bill and Harmony can find a way to coexist peacefully. I have come to the decision that it is necessary for me to end my relationship with Billy. It is important to appreciate life while we have it. As

Harmony discusses Mahogany, it is clear that I do not take shortcuts. It is easy to assume that everyone around us is content and has it all together, but that is often not the case. Harmony, you are right in saying that you have not experienced the challenges I have faced in my life.

There have been moments when I felt lost and overwhelmed. I have reached out for support, only to be met with judgment instead of understanding. Despite being labeled as crazy, I have taken steps to address my issues. I have sought therapy to work through my struggles, including my relationship with Musa. I am committed to achieving my goals and finding happiness for myself. I could have lost my insanity. a moment of realization that my actions were not only affecting me but also my children. My therapist helped me see that I was putting my health at risk and potentially causing harm to myself. It was a wake-up call for me to start appreciating life a little more.

I now understand that my children can sense my pain and stress, and it can have a negative impact on them. I can see how my oldest son was affected by witnessing the abuse I endured from his father. It breaks my heart to think that he was exposed to such violence at a young age and how it affected him.

Last weekend, we were both doing something silly and eating something we shouldn't have. It was a scary moment that made me realize how fragile life is. I could have lost my mind that day, and it was a wake-up call for me to start taking better care of myself and my children. Life is too precious to take for granted. . While seated in a chair, I found myself contemplating the state of my mindset, which seemed clouded, resulting in double vision and auditory hallucinations. This episode lasted approximately an hour, causing increasing fear as the symptoms intensified. In moments like these, it is easy to focus on trivial complaints, forgetting the abundance of blessings we have such as our mental faculties, shelter, sustenance, clothing, and employment, even if it may not align with our ideal expectations in terms of job satisfaction or financial remuneration.

Reflecting on my past employment experiences, I choose not to dwell on negativity, as ultimately, the decision to remain in a particular role was mine. It is essential for us, as individuals, to take responsibility for our own growth and strive to transform our perspective for the better. One effective practice is to write down our aspirations daily, followed by reading them aloud each morning. By visualizing and affirming our desires, such as owning a home or property, we can manifest our dreams into reality.

As I share these thoughts with you, Mahogany, I implore you to consider the power of committing your goals to writing. The act of writing serves as a tangible reminder of our aspirations and can serve as a catalyst for positive change in our lives. Remember, it is through intentional action and unwavering determination that we can transform our visions into tangible achievements. What's going on? Well, for the past few years, we haven't been talking. I experienced difficulties in my life when I met this guy, whose name was Hawaii. I left my whole house for him. believe that everything is going to happen. I believe that God will provide me with everything I have been thinking about. Prayer has the power to change everything. Mahogany, I make a habit of writing down my goals - to live debt-free, pay off my car and house, graduate, make the list, get a new job, and achieve all that I desire. I write it down, pray for it, and it comes to fruition. You are a source of goodness for others!!! You are blessed, even if you may not realize it. Remember to prioritize yourself. Self-preservation is crucial. Write down your goals and aspirations. Mahogany, I lay everything out on the table. How are things going in your life at the moment? Jamaica sounds like a place of relaxation and enjoyment. Let's keep our conversations about Jamaica private. As for me, we have not been in touch for a few years. I faced challenges when I met a man named Hawaii, and I made significant sacrifices for him. My son Harmony and I went through a period of hardship. It seems like you may have experienced something similar. I wanted to give her the same love I gave my children, but there was always controversy with that one. I have not yet reached that particular juncture. Our journey began with Hawaii. My mother frequently imparted the wisdom that one truly understands a person only upon living with them. Indeed, the true nature of Hawaii was revealed.

His true character was exposed when I arrived. To my surprise, I discovered that he had a child, a charming little girl. However, the backstory revealed that the child's mother was a woman struggling with addiction, grappling with the harsh realities of life on the streets. I refrained from probing further. I grew deeply fond of the child, who seemed to yearn for a maternal presence in her life. As a mother of three, I desired to shower her with the same love I bestowed upon my own children. However, complications arose. Hawaii consistently intervened, ensuring that no emotional bond was formed. From dawn until dusk, he consistently initiated conflicts in the late hours of the night. Despite the fact that the baby was well-behaved, I found myself awake in the morning not because of her, but because of his actions. It was evident that he truly had no desire to engage with me. I had to come to terms with that reality. My confusion stemmed from the question of why he would go to such lengths to provoke jealousy in another woman, causing me to leave my home. If he had been honest about his intentions, I could have handled the situation differently and avoided forming any emotional attachments. Enduring difficult circumstances has allowed me to reflect on the challenges I have faced. I am grateful that you reached out to me, as I had disconnected myself and lost your contact information. Regardless of the circumstances, I am pleased to see you and appreciate your call. Your gesture means a great deal to me. I always had faith that you would be there for me. Much love. Moving forward, it is important for us to focus on the future rather than dwelling on the past. It is beneficial to keep each other informed of our experiences in order to improve our lives and financial stability. It is essential that we prioritize self-love as the foundation for our growth and success.

I am currently supporting Musa, although recent events have made me reconsider the nature of our relationship. I believe it is best to maintain a friendship moving forward.

Let us make the most of this vacation and relax with a glass of wine, as long as it does not harm our well-being. I am also navigating the complexities of my pregnancy and the situation with Musa. Reflecting on recent events has provided me with valuable insights that he may not be aware of. The environment in which he placed me, observing from the outside and waiting for the inevitable chaos to unfold, is rapidly deteriorating. It is causing a significant awakening among many individuals. Musa's true sexual orientation has been revealed, as witnessed by his intimate interactions with another man. This revelation has prompted a surprised reaction from Mahogany, who expressed disbelief. Regardless of Musa's feelings for Harmony, Mahogany remains unconcerned, focusing instead on the impending birth of their child following their recent trip to Jamaica. Now that the child has been born, a doctor has informed Harmony and Musa that they must undergo testing for Chlamydia. This news sparked a heated argument between the two, with Musa feeling unfairly targeted as the potential carrier of the infection. Amidst the tension, accusations were hurled back and forth, with Musa questioning Harmony's past relationships. It is clear that there are unresolved issues that need to be addressed. I was on vacation in Jamaica. I did a lot of thinking. All you ever wanted to do was to have a good time, but unfortunately, you got caught up in some trouble. Your actions have led to serious consequences, as I have contracted chlamydia from you. It is important that you are honest and upfront about your mistakes. There are things about you that I am aware of, which you may not even realize. I am giving you an opportunity to come clean with me now. I am choosing to walk away from this situation. It is your responsibility to take care of the child that has been born as a result of our actions. It is clear to me that you are old enough to know right from wrong. I believed that you were ready to be open and honest with me, but it seems that you are not prepared for a serious relationship. It is important to have honest and open communication when we are alone together. During my recent vacation in Jamaica, I had time to reflect on our situation. I have come to the conclusion that you are not ready for a committed relationship. I was quite surprised by recent revelations. I never expected Musa to be bisexual, but the reality is apparent. Musa, there is no room for dishonesty, as I have witnessed actions that confirm this truth. While we may not be able to continue our relationship, it is imperative that you take responsibility for the child we will be raising together. Our connection runs deep, and I am committed to our shared investments. Walking away from our history is not an option, but moving forward as a couple is unlikely. It is clear that there have been misunderstandings and false pretenses. Musa, it is time to be honest and acknowledge your true self. Additionally, I must disclose that I am also bisexual, further complicating the situation. Despite these revelations, my feelings for you remain genuine and unwavering. Your approach to expressing love is unconventional. Love should make me feel like royalty, on top of the world. I must admit, you do provide me with everything I desire and more, for which I am grateful. However, I value my worth as a woman and aim to embody the qualities of a Proverbs 31 woman, as my grandmother taught me. With that said, Musa, I will be taking a step back for now and plan to return in five years. During my absence, my children will oversee the RV park. I will stay in touch periodically and will speak with you before I depart. I have no intention of tarnishing your reputation, so I choose to gracefully exit the situation. We will talk again soon. Please take care of our child. I encourage you to spend less time gaming and being insincere. Rest assured, I will be in contact with Billy covertly. During the time spent in his personal space, he expressed a desire for assistance in developing a plan to explore and potentially change his sexual orientation and behavior. Uncertainty regarding attraction to individuals of either gender was acknowledged. In response, a comprehensive plan incorporating positive and negative reinforcement strategies is recommended. The plan should outline clear circumstances and objectives, ensuring accountability and progress tracking.

Positive reinforcement techniques will be utilized to reward desired behaviors and progress, while negative reinforcement will discourage undesired actions. Regular communication and support will be provided to maintain motivation and focus. It is important to establish a routine and set achievable goals to facilitate progress.

As we navigate this journey together, it is essential to consider the impact on our lives and future decisions. While the path forward may be uncertain, the investment in personal growth and self-discovery is invaluable. Temporary separation may be necessary to allow for individual reflection and growth. Despite any challenges, our friendship and professional partnership will endure.

In addition to exploring new interests, creating a daily to-do list can help maintain structure and productivity. By prioritizing self-care and personal development, we can navigate this process with intention and purpose. Your commitment to caring for our shared responsibilities, such as our child, is appreciated and respected.

Together, we will navigate this transformative period with resilience and compassion, embracing the opportunity for personal growth and self-discovery. It is important to consider changing your daily routine by engaging in different activities. As a form of positive reinforcement, I recommend reducing the amount of time spent playing video games in order to address behavior patterns related to inappropriate content and excessive screen time. While it may be tempting to continue gaming for long periods twice a week, it is not a healthy habit to maintain. It is crucial to establish positive habits through self-rewarding behavior instead.

It is best to avoid spending excessive time in isolation with technology, as it can lead to a breakdown in trust and communication. Being transparent about personal preferences and boundaries from the beginning is essential in maintaining healthy relationships. In the given scenario, it is clear that miscommunication and lack of honesty have caused a breach of trust. It is important to acknowledge and address these issues in order to move forward positively. I struggled to understand the complexities of relationships, as I was distracted by materialistic pursuits that hindered my ability to truly love.

Keywords:

1. Aristocratic district
2. Money getting red
3. Luxurious lifestyles
4. Inner strength
5. Self-worth
6. Phenomenal women
7. Life challenges
8. Finding values
9. Friendship
10. Striving for a better life

My Journal Planner | Day 1

My Journal Planner | Day 2

My Journal Planner | Day 3

My Journal Planner | Day 4

My Journal Planner | Day 5

My Journal Planner | Day 6

My Journal Planner | Day 7

My Journal Planner | Day 8

My Journal Planner | Day 9

My Journal Planner | Day 10

My Journal Planner | Day 11

My Journal Planner | Day 12

My Journal Planner | Day 13

My Journal Planner | Day 14

My Journal Planner | Day 15

My Journal Planner | Day 16

My Journal Planner | Day 17

My Journal Planner | Day 18

My Journal Planner | Day 19

My Journal Planner | Day 20

My Journal Planner | Day 21

My Journal Planner | Day 22

My Journal Planner | Day 23

My Journal Planner | Day 24

My Journal Planner | Day 25

My Journal Planner | Day 26

My Journal Planner | Day 27

My Journal Planner | Day 28

My Journal Planner | Day 29

My Journal Planner | Day 30

www.ingramcontent.com/pod-product-compliance
Lightning Source LLC
LaVergne TN
LVHW052002060526
838201LV00059B/3802